5 GIRAFFES

Anne Innis Dagg

Fitzhenry & Whiteside

Published in Canada by Fitzhenry & Whiteside,
195 Allstate Parkway, Markham, ON L3R 4T8

Published in the United States by Fitzhenry & Whiteside,
311 Washington Street, Brighton, Massachusetts 02135

10 9 8 7 6 5 4 3 2 1

Fitzhenry & Whiteside acknowledges with thanks the Canada Council for the Arts,
and the Ontario Arts Council for their support of our publishing program.

We acknowledge the financial support of the Government of Canada for our publishing activities.

Funded by the Government of Canada  Canada

 ONTARIO ARTS COUNCIL
CONSEIL DES ARTS DE L'ONTARIO
an Ontario government agency
un organisme du gouvernement de l'Ontario

 Canada Council   Conseil des arts
for the Arts   du Canada

Library and Archives Canada Cataloguing in Publication
Dagg, Anne Innis, 1933-, author
5 giraffes / Anne Innis Dagg.
Includes bibliographical references and index.

ISBN 978-1-55455-356-3 (bound)

1. Giraffes--Biography--Juvenile literature. 2. Giraffes--
Juvenile literature. I. Title. II. Title: Five giraffes.
QL737.U56D343 2016   j599.638092'9   C2014-907183-3

Publisher Cataloging-in-Publication Data (U.S.)
Names: Dagg, Anne Innis, author.
Title: 5 giraffes / Anne Innis Dagg.

Other titles: Five giraffes.
Description: Markham, Ontario : Fitzhenry & Whiteside Limited, 2016.
Includes bibliographical references and index. |Summary: "The latest in the 5 Animals series,
with an introduction by Rob Laidlaw, 5 Giraffes profiles five unique giraffes from both
captivity and the wild. Accompanying the five giraffe profiles are chapters about their diet,
social life, and the giraffe's unusual body" – Provided by publisher.

Identifiers: ISBN 8-1-55455-356-3 (hardcover)
Subjects: LCSH: Giraffe—Juvenile literature. | BISAC: JUVENILE NONFICTION / Animals / Giraffes.
Classification: LCC QL737.U56D334 |DDC 599.638 – dc23

Text and cover design by Tanya Montini
Printed in China by Sheck Wah Tong Printing Press Ltd.

CONTENTS

DEDICATION

To Tiffany Soechting and to Buddy,
the first giraffe I ever touched.
June 2014

ACKNOWLEDGEMENTS

Ashley Arimborgo
Douglas Bolger
Lisa Clifton-Bumpass
Kerryn Carter
Liza Dadone
Chris Darbishire
John Doherty
Susan Gow
Sheri Horiszny
Solange Messier
Erica Meyer
Anne Miner
Zoe Muller
Jason Pootoolal
Amy Schilz
Tiffany Soechting
Jean Stevenson
Heather Wilson

FOREWORD

Anne Innis Dagg's fascination with giraffes began when she was just a toddler. After she saw giraffes in a zoo, she knew she would study these amazing animals in the wild one day. So, after graduating from university in 1955 with a Gold Medal in Biology, Anne made the daring decision to travel from her native Canada to Africa on her own to conduct a study of the behaviour of giraffes in their natural habitat. No one had ever done anything like that before. Now she is a well-known animal rights advocate, scientist, teacher, and the author of many scientific papers, articles, and books. She is also the first person to have studied a large mammal—the giraffe—in the wilds of Africa.

Everyone knows giraffes. Babies have toy stuffed giraffes to play with, women wear scarves featuring their spotting, and popular children's animated films, such as *Madagascar*, depict them as characters. But few people know that giraffes in the world are becoming endangered. If something is not done soon to protect them, they are headed for extinction.

Anne arrived in South Africa, after a three-week-long ship voyage, in the summer of 1956. She spent the next year studying giraffes in the wild, often watching them from early morning until sunset. When she first started, little was known about the natural behaviours and lifestyles of giraffes, but Anne's field studies and research changed all that. Her research also helped establish her as one of the world's leading giraffe experts.

5 Giraffes is an important book and it comes at an important time. In the last fifteen years, poaching and the presence of humans into giraffe habitats have significantly reduced Africa's total giraffe population. Today there are fewer than 80,000 giraffes left on the entire African continent. Some giraffe populations have suffered even more drastic declines, such as the giraffes of Kenya's Maasai Mara National Reserve, and all over the world, giraffes in captivity face challenges of their own, such as poor living conditions, foot problems, and inbreeding.

In recent years, a great deal of well-deserved attention has been focused on the plight of elephants and rhinos, but we should not forget about Africa's giraffes. While they are popular and easily recognizable to most people, they are often overlooked. *5 Giraffes* will help bring attention to these incredible animals and the challenges they now face. But more importantly, it will encourage readers to get involved in helping giraffes. So, read on, learn, and become inspired so that you, too, can play a role in ensuring that giraffes remain a part of our lives and the African landscape forever.

Rob Laidlaw
Animal Activist
Executive Director, Zoocheck

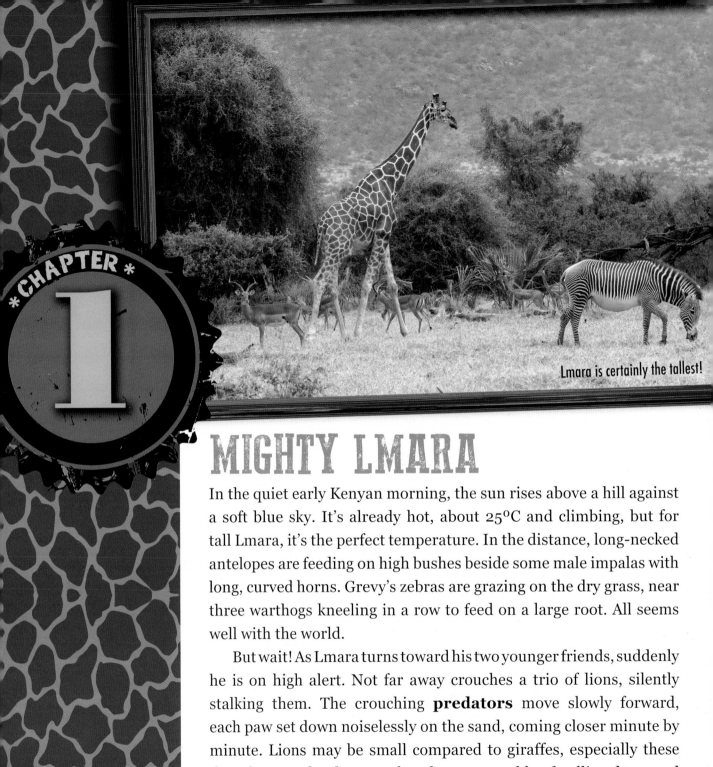

Lmara is certainly the tallest!

CHAPTER 1

MIGHTY LMARA

In the quiet early Kenyan morning, the sun rises above a hill against a soft blue sky. It's already hot, about 25°C and climbing, but for tall Lmara, it's the perfect temperature. In the distance, long-necked antelopes are feeding on high bushes beside some male impalas with long, curved horns. Grevy's zebras are grazing on the dry grass, near three warthogs kneeling in a row to feed on a large root. All seems well with the world.

But wait! As Lmara turns toward his two younger friends, suddenly he is on high alert. Not far away crouches a trio of lions, silently stalking them. The crouching **predators** move slowly forward, each paw set down noiselessly on the sand, coming closer minute by minute. Lions may be small compared to giraffes, especially these three large males, but together they are capable of pulling down and killing Lmara or one of his buddies.

Suddenly, as if at a given signal, the giraffes turn as one and flee on their long legs, heading up the hill, away from their feeding grounds beside the river. The lions turn on the speed and race after

Lmara galloping away.

Grevy's zebras are a type of zebra with thin black stripes.

them, the air now thick with sand thrown up by **hooves** and paws. Lion attacks are real risks on **reserves**, but luckily the three giraffes escape without a scratch.

Lmara and his friends are reticulated giraffes. Many people think the reticulated giraffes in Samburu are the most beautiful in Africa. Unlike the blotchy skin patterns of other types of giraffes, their skin patterns are like creamy white lines on a rich red-brown coat—rather like netting, which is what the word *reticulated* means.

Four-legged animals aren't the only creatures awake in the Samburu National Reserve this morning. Watching the drama from afar are John Doherty, a **biologist** who heads the Reticulated Giraffe Project, and Jacob Leaidura, a local **naturalist** of the Samburu tribe who was born in the area. Their goal is to preserve the reticulated giraffes in the Samburu National Reserve in northern Kenya.

It is difficult to tell the giraffes apart since all have large brown spots that look similar in pattern. In order for John to identify each individual, he tries to find a marking on the giraffe's body that isn't found on any other giraffe. Lmara has a mark that looks like a trident—a spear with three prongs. If you look closely, you can see the three unusual white lines on the right side of his lower neck.

The coat of
a reticulated giraffe.

The circled "trident" identifies Lmara.

A female giraffe's ossicones.

Lmara is unique because of the trident pattern, but also because of the distinctive horns on his head. These aren't horns like those of cows and antelopes, but rather bony growths sometimes called **ossicones**, which at first are covered with skin and topped with black hairs. Adult females have two horns, but adult males may develop as many as five. The male's main pair of horns is usually hairless on top because the hair is rubbed off in the frequent fighting matches that they have as they grow up. Other bony structures often develop on the heads of males, too. Lmara has a new growth slowly forming over his left eye.

When Lmara was old enough to leave his mother, he joined other young males who spent most of the day just hanging out. He often scuffled with one of his friends, the two of them standing side by side and swinging their heads so that, with alternate blows, their horns hit each other. As they grew older and stronger, their fights became more serious. Eventually all of the youngsters knew enough to stay clear of the fiercest combatants, like Lmara. They retreated from a group of giraffes if Lmara joined it. These most powerful males are the ones who **mate** with the females.

By the time Lmara was seven years old, he was fully grown— about 4.9 metres (16 feet) tall and about 1,200 kilograms (2,645 pounds) in weight. Now, like typical adult male giraffes, he is often a loner, spending much of his time **browsing** for food, reaching up as high as 5.5 metres (18 feet) to snatch leaves from a tall acacia tree or bending his neck down to feed on low shrubs. Each day he eats as much as 34 kilograms (75 pounds) of leaves. He also spends time resting now and then, bringing up partly digested food from his first stomach to chew on. This system works well because he can eat in a hurry in areas where he might be in danger, and then chew the food again later, in a safer area. How lucky he is, compared to captive giraffes, to be able to eat his fill of many different kinds of leaves each day. Like other large males, Lmara is a great walker. When he isn't feeding, he often walks long distances to join groups of females. Lmara is one-third bigger than full-grown females, with a coat that is becoming darker as he ages.

Lmara lives the life of a truly free giraffe in Africa. He can roam in huge areas without ever encountering a fence. While he may never know it, Lmara has a fortunate life on the reserve. Unlike many captive giraffes, Lmara does not suffer from cold **climates**, cramped living spaces, limited companions, or the many health problems associated with captive life. However, wild giraffes in Africa face other problems.

Fifteen years ago, there were about 30,000 reticulated giraffes in Africa, but now fewer than 5,000 remain. Many fear that this race of giraffe may soon go **extinct** in the wild. The main reason for this is that they are eaten, not by lions, although that does happen, but by hunters who trap or shoot them illegally to sell their meat. To the north and east of Samburu are **war-torn areas** where millions of people live in desperate conditions without much food. Many people in these areas have high-powered guns with which to kill people or animals. And those driven from their homes into survival camps need food to eat. Near where Lmara lives, more than twelve million people displaced from their homes are hungry and eager to have **bush meat**. Here, most **poachers** use heavy guns to kill animals for their meat. But killing and eating all the giraffes and other wild animals is not the solution. It is vital, instead, that governments help their people so that they do not have to depend on the meat of animals killed illegally.

Many countries have wildlife rangers who work to protect giraffes and other wildlife from poachers. This is especially true in nations where tourism is a major source of income, such as in Kenya and Tanzania. However, these rangers are often poorly paid, with their lives in danger from armed poachers determined to kill animals so that they can make money from selling their meat. Greater measures need to be taken to protect these giraffes before we lose them forever.

Lmara browsing for food.

Brave rangers try to protect giraffes from danger.

A group of giraffes browsing.

FOOD—A TALL ORDER OF LEAVES

Unlike most large **herbivores**, giraffes don't eat grass. Rather, they eat the leaves of as many as ninety **species** of bushes and trees. Where do giraffes live in Africa? They live wherever there are bushes and trees for them to eat. Giraffes in reserves also eat leaves from many kinds of trees and bushes, unlike in zoos, where their diet is supplemented with food, like cabbage.

Male and female giraffes have different feeding behaviours. Because the males are larger than the females, they need more food. They often eat the leaves high up on the trees where there is no competition from the shorter females. By doing this, they can also keep an eye out for the approach of competing males. As well, females with young may feed differently than females without offspring. Mothers and their young tend to stay in more open areas, eating whatever leaves are available there. In open areas, they can see if there are lions in the distance and flee if needed.

Because of their height, giraffes are able to live entirely on the leaves of trees and bushes. Most other large **mammals** spend their

The colour of a giraffe's tongue is a blackish blue or purple with a pink base. The darker colour in the front is thought to protect the giraffe's tongue from getting sunburned.

days grazing on grass rather than browsing in trees. Giraffes need a lot of protein in their diets, and grass doesn't provide as much protein as the leaves of bushes and trees do. By eating these highly nutritious leaves, female giraffes are healthy enough to become pregnant at any time of the year. By contrast, large mammals, such as buffaloes, zebras, and wildebeests, which eat only grass, give birth only during or shortly after the rainy season when there is plenty of vegetation to eat. That is when the mothers eat well enough to produce ample milk.

Oddly enough, although plants seem passive, they have ways of fighting back to reduce the amount of time that hungry animals feast on them. Giraffes are the main feeders on vegetation high above the ground, and by eating it, they have apparently moulded the very form of some of their favourite trees. Some are shaped rather like umbrellas, with most of their leaves in a flat, circular mass at the top of the tree trunk. Giraffes feed easily at the outer edge of this flat crown, but the tree has several advantages. For one thing, the giraffes can't eat as much of the

The acacia tree.

Stinging ants on a plant.

vegetation as they would if the leaves could readily be eaten at every level. Also, the leaves are positioned in such a way that they receive maximum exposure to the sun. This allows them to grow rapidly. Some tree species favoured by giraffes grow thorns or hooks on their branches, which hinder animals from feeding on them. Fortunately for the giraffes, they have furry lips and a mobile tongue that is 45 centimetres (18 inches) long and can work around the thorns to pluck up the tasty leaves. Researchers decided to study these thorns because they had noticed that some acacia trees had longer thorns than others. They found that the thorns were shorter on the branches that were too high for giraffes to reach and on trees near the research station where giraffes did not venture. The trees that were more often grazed by giraffes were the ones with the longest thorns.

Other trees fight back by encouraging stinging ants to live on them. These trees develop small pads at the base of leaf stems called nectaries, which contain nectar-like honey that ants love. In this way, the trees provide both room and board for the insects. As their name implies, stinging ants sting when they are disturbed, rushing to attack the head of any giraffe that is munching on their branch. Large giraffes usually put up with this discomfort, although they

A giraffe browsing on a short bush.

often leave to find another less painful source of food. However, when feeding youngsters are attacked by stinging ants, they may suddenly stop eating and leap back, violently snorting and shaking their heads, trying to get rid of the ants.

Trees favoured by giraffes, such as acacias, may produce chemicals in their tissues, such as tannins, cyanide, and prussic acid, in an attempt to discourage hungry giraffes. Tannins taste bad and are harmful. They reduce the amount of protein giraffes can receive from the leaves. In Niger, female giraffes that are nursing their young actively avoid eating leaves rich in tannins.

Giraffes also enjoy eating the high blossoms of flowering trees and while they may lean down and seem to be eating grass, they are actually eating a low plant, such as the prickly pear cactus, instead. Sometimes giraffes reach down to lick or bite salty soil or to pick up bones to chew, usually in the dry season when the vegetation is less nutritious. This is called **pica behaviour**. The bones provide them with nutritious elements, such as calcium and phosphorus, for their diets.

Giraffes thrive on the leaves of different species of trees and bushes. This ability has allowed them to spread into huge new areas of Africa over many thousands of years.

A mother and her calf.

CHAPTER 3

THE EVOLUTION OF GIRAFFES

Now that you know what giraffes eat, you probably think it's obvious why they have such long necks—to reach the leafy treetops, right? They can reach much higher than other leaf-eaters, with the exception, of course, of small animals, such as monkeys, who often feed in trees. Most scientists used to believe this was the reason for giraffes' long necks. It is a neat, simple **theory**.

Unfortunately, it seems this theory is wrong. There had always been problems with this belief. For example, why did a giraffe need to be 4.9 metres (16 feet) tall? Giraffes that are only 3 metres (10 feet) tall could still take advantage of food unavailable to other large mammals. Why did giraffes often choose to browse on low bushes despite having to bend over to do so? And why were the heads of males so much heavier than those of females?

The new theory is that giraffes **evolved** to have long necks because females preferred to mate with tall males who had stronger necks than their rivals. Researchers who watch giraffes in the wild know that even young males like to spend time fighting with other

Zarafa zelteni

Samotherium maurusium

Okapia johnstoni

Giraffa jumae

Some of the early ancestors of giraffes.

males, as did young Lmara and his friends. As males grow larger and stronger, they fight each other more fiercely. Now these taller long-necked winners, like Lmara, become the fathers of the new generation of youngsters—with long necks, just like Dad's.

Early **ancestors** of giraffes living in Asia, called giraffids, did not have long necks. The males of these relatives had horns on the sides of their heads, indicating that they did not fight the way most large mammals did. Male rams, for example, have heavy horns over their foreheads and fight by running at each other and crashing their foreheads together to see which one is most able to withstand the shock. Moose and elk have antlers with many spikes. When these males fight, their antlers intertwine as they push and twist against each other to determine which male is strongest. Giraffe ancestors were different; the position of their small horns indicated that they fought from the side, not from the front.

The necks of giraffe ancestors that had moved into Africa began to get longer about twelve million years ago, according to fossil bones found in various parts of Africa. Those males with strong, longer necks were at an advantage in fighting matches, because they could swing their heads and horns with greater force to hit the bodies of their opponents. The winners were the ones who did most of the mating, so gradually, over many generations, the necks of these giraffids grew longer. The earliest bones of the giraffes we know today, *Giraffa camelopardalis*, date from the late **Pliocene period** about three million years ago, and were found in the country of Chad in north central Africa.

Giraffe ancestors migrated to Africa from Asia by way of what is now Ethiopia. Gradually, as new giraffid species, including the

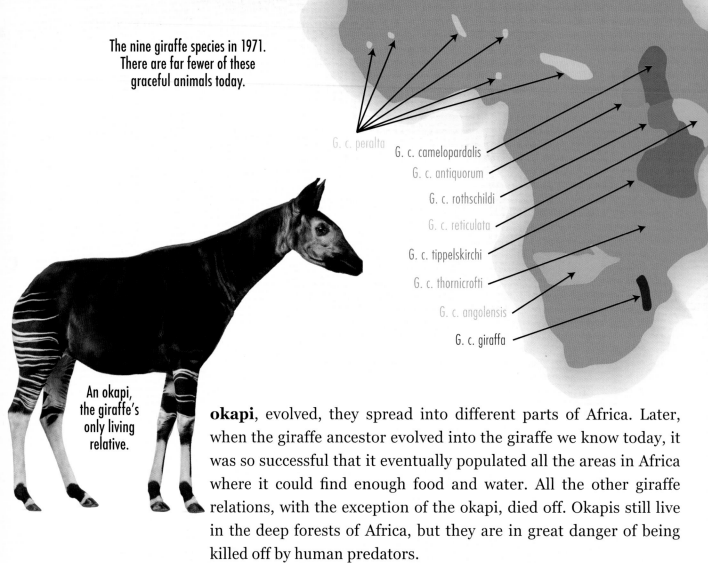

The nine giraffe species in 1971. There are far fewer of these graceful animals today.

G. c. peralta
G. c. camelopardalis
G. c. antiquorum
G. c. rothschildi
G. c. reticulata
G. c. tippelskirchi
G. c. thornicrofti
G. c. angolensis
G. c. giraffa

An okapi, the giraffe's only living relative.

okapi, evolved, they spread into different parts of Africa. Later, when the giraffe ancestor evolved into the giraffe we know today, it was so successful that it eventually populated all the areas in Africa where it could find enough food and water. All the other giraffe relations, with the exception of the okapi, died off. Okapis still live in the deep forests of Africa, but they are in great danger of being killed off by human predators.

When a species spreads out over a huge area, as happened gradually with giraffes in Africa, different populations become separated and no longer have contact with each other. In time, perhaps with changes in climate, these populations evolve into different races, also called subspecies. This is what has happened to giraffes. Now there are nine giraffe subspecies living in different parts of Africa. Some of the groups are small in number, so they are in danger of extinction. Several races, such as the reticulated giraffes like Lmara, have distinctive coats so that their race is easy to recognize. But giraffes from most races have similar spotting so that it is impossible to tell them apart just by looking at them.

If giraffes from most races look about the same, why does the extinction of one of the races matter? It matters because each race has distinct **DNA**. It has taken sometimes more than a million years for a race to develop, and it would be devastating for science if we lost even one of them. There is still so much to learn about each subspecies of giraffe. We don't even know if giraffes of different races behave differently—not enough studies have been done in the wild. The number of wild *Giraffa camelopardalis peralta* giraffes in Niger and Rothschild's giraffes in East Africa are already so low that they have been listed in the **endangered category** by the International Union for the Conservation of Nature.

A Thornicroft's giraffe

Although a male giraffe from one race could easily walk for long distances each day, and after a few days reach and mate with females of a different race, they virtually never do. For example, Thornicroft's giraffes in Zambia live only about 400 kilometres (248 miles) from Tippelskirch's giraffes in Tanzania, but they have not **interbred**, even though there are no mountains or large rivers that separate their two homes. It seems to be because no male wants to go far away from the other giraffes he is familiar with.

Until recently, we did not have any genetic information on giraffes. Getting giraffe DNA in the wild is difficult, but some experts have been able to retrieve it. Zoos throughout the world take DNA findings seriously. In the past, they often did not know where the giraffes in their collections came from. They may have been sent long ago by boat to England or the United States with papers stating only that they were from Africa. A giraffe was a giraffe. It had not seemed important. Now, giraffes in captivity are no longer allowed to **breed** if they belong to different subspecies. Many zoos still have giraffes from different races in their zoos, but each subspecies is kept strictly apart from another to prevent mating.

The International Union for the Conservation of Nature (IUCN) is the oldest and largest organization dedicated to protecting natural resources and biodiversity, including giraffe subspecies!

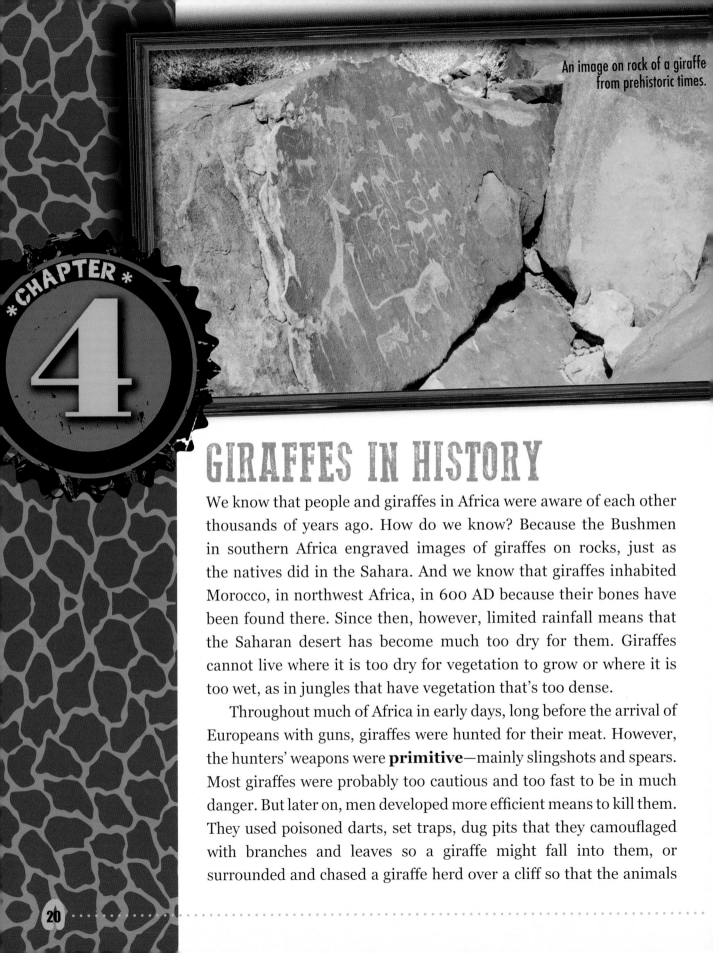

An image on rock of a giraffe from prehistoric times.

CHAPTER 4

GIRAFFES IN HISTORY

We know that people and giraffes in Africa were aware of each other thousands of years ago. How do we know? Because the Bushmen in southern Africa engraved images of giraffes on rocks, just as the natives did in the Sahara. And we know that giraffes inhabited Morocco, in northwest Africa, in 600 AD because their bones have been found there. Since then, however, limited rainfall means that the Saharan desert has become much too dry for them. Giraffes cannot live where it is too dry for vegetation to grow or where it is too wet, as in jungles that have vegetation that's too dense.

Throughout much of Africa in early days, long before the arrival of Europeans with guns, giraffes were hunted for their meat. However, the hunters' weapons were **primitive**—mainly slingshots and spears. Most giraffes were probably too cautious and too fast to be in much danger. But later on, men developed more efficient means to kill them. They used poisoned darts, set traps, dug pits that they camouflaged with branches and leaves so a giraffe might fall into them, or surrounded and chased a giraffe herd over a cliff so that the animals would fall to their deaths. When men riding on camels or on horses arrived on the scene, however, giraffes were in far more danger. These animals could chase them until the giraffes collapsed.

A dead giraffe provided a huge quantity of meat, but its body parts were also useful to people. The long leg **tendons** could be made into guitar or bow strings, or used for sewing. The tough hide could be made into a shield, or into buckets, pots, drum covers, whips, or sandals. The long tail could become a **fly switch**, or individual hairs could be fashioned into thread, necklaces, or bracelets. People were not wasteful of the giraffes they hunted, and overhunting was not a concern before guns were invented.

A suitcase fashioned "à la girafe."

Giraffes did not live as far north as Egypt, so there must have been great excitement when one was transported there as early as 2,500 BC. A few individual giraffes continued to be brought north over the years to satisfy rich Egyptians who wanted them as status symbols.

In 46 AD, the first giraffe reached Europe and was presented to Julius Caesar in Rome as a gift from Cleopatra. Again there was much fuss over this new creature. Being big like a camel with spots like a leopard, it was called a cameleopard. This word is incorporated in the scientific name for the giraffe, *Giraffa camelopardalis*. The generic name *Giraffa* comes from the Arabic word *xirapha*, meaning "one who walks swiftly."

More recently, in 1827, a young giraffe captured in Africa was shipped to France. Townspeople were so excited that some created new fashions "à la girafe," with dresses decorated with spots and handbags made in the colour of the giraffe's coat. The king was so delighted that he allowed the giraffe to eat rose petals from his hand. The giraffe lived in the Paris Zoo for seventeen years before she died.

The British were annoyed that the French had a giraffe and they did not. So in 1836, King William IV hired a Frenchman to go to Africa to capture a giraffe for Britain. The man caught four young giraffes and shipped them off to the king. They, too, caused excitement when they were marched through London to the Regent Park Zoo. The poor animals had been cooped up for so long on the boat that when they spotted the leafy trees, they were wild with excitement, kicking out with their legs and waving their necks. The men supervising the giraffes could barely control them. The animals were eventually lured into the elephant house with bits of sugar. This was to be their home for the next year, as it was the only structure tall and roomy enough to suit them. A giraffe house was eventually built for them, where they and their offspring lived for many years. The last of those giraffes died in 1881.

In the days before movies and television, watching unusual animals in zoos was an exciting pastime that drew great crowds. Business people began **importing** animals into Europe on a large scale. From 1866 to 1886, a German businessman called Carl Hagenbeck imported 150 giraffes to Europe. Soon giraffes were also being sent to other countries around the world to be kept in captivity.

A hunter on horseback chasing giraffes.

In the 1800s and early 1900s, Europeans and Americans began to stream into Africa, bringing guns with them. **Game hunters** shot thousands of giraffes in the name of sport, chasing after them on horseback. Soon, in both South Africa and East Africa, many people feared that giraffe subspecies living in those areas would be completely destroyed by humans.

Fortunately, some people fought to stop this **massacre**. In 1913, a few game reserves were set aside where giraffes and other wild animals could be safe, and in 1933, a first Conference for the Protection of the Fauna and Flora of Africa was held in London to discuss how to protect the giraffes. It was now seen as wrong to kill an animal for no reason.

Today, although virtually all giraffes in Africa are protected by law, the danger of races becoming extinct is greater than ever. The number of people in Africa is growing fast, which means more food is needed to feed people and more space is being taken up. Giraffes are killed illegally at night to be sold for meat, and fences trap them or keep them from getting food. Giraffe numbers are declining, so it is important to do what we can to ensure all the races of giraffe survive in Africa.

Safari at four and a half months still loves milk.

CHAPTER 5

YOUNG SAFARI

Safari is one of a kind. She was born and lives at the African Lion Safari near Cambridge, Ontario, in Canada, and she looks like any other young giraffe. In reality, even though she may not realize it, she is an important member of a scientific research team. The information her team collects may help endangered races of giraffe survive in the wild.

Safari is famous because she is a kind of "test tube baby." Her mother, named Calgary, had been treated by **artificial insemination**. A male giraffe, Jimmy, donated sperm, which was implanted in Calgary's uterus. Safari was the first infant to be born in Canada using this treatment, and the second in the whole world.

On the very last day of 2013, baby Safari dropped from her mother into the world from a height of nearly two metres (6 feet). She weighed a healthy 60 kilograms (132 pounds) and already stood 1.75 metres (5.7 feet) tall, once she managed to rise on her wobbly legs. She was already as tall as some of the people caring for her in the barn!

Head giraffe keeper Jason Pootoolal, who is in charge of the team, was particularly thrilled. He has collected extensive reproductive

Giraffe calves should be cared for by their mothers when possible.

information related to her birth, which will be published and used by many other scientists who are anxious to help preserve giraffes.

The giraffe team was excited over this new addition to its herd but Calgary, who had never before given birth, was confused about this new creature that had suddenly appeared. She did not lick her baby or allow her to suckle. Because she was living under unnatural conditions in captivity, her **maternal instincts** were likely not strong, and she failed to give her **calf** the proper attention she needed. In order to make sure Safari was as healthy as possible, the keepers decided to help Calgary bring up her youngster. Although experts all agree that it's better for an infant to be raised by its mother, as it is in the wild, many giraffes have been raised by hand.

The staff did a wonderful job of bringing up Safari. When she was six months old, she was already 2.56 metres (8.4 feet) tall and weighed 212 kilograms (467 pounds). Every few hours she was gulping down cow's milk from a large bottle. In fact, she was drinking ten litres (21 pints) of milk a day.

Ten adult giraffes share their large spread of rolling grasslands, scattered trees, and a lake with young Safari. Their home is much larger than a zoo, but it's still small for a large mammal that has unlimited space in the wild or 40,000 acres (16,187 hectares) on an average reserve. Every day when it's warm, the giraffes are let out of their barn to wander among the other herbivores, such as wild sheep, wildebeests, and rhinoceroses. There are certainly not enough leaves from bushes and trees to feed the giraffes, so cut branches, carrots, lettuce, and other foods are placed in high containers for them. Staff must make sure to monitor their diets carefully because captive giraffes have died from lack of proper food. Some types of leaves, such as those from oleander trees, are actually poisonous and must never be given to giraffes. A diet high

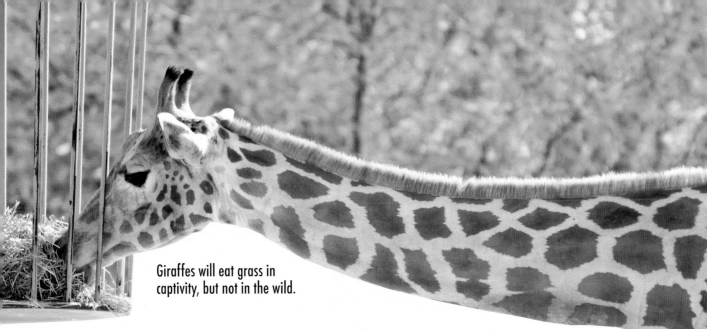

Giraffes will eat grass in captivity, but not in the wild.

in grains can also kill them. In captivity, giraffes never receive the varied diets that they would otherwise have in the wild.

When the giraffes return to the barn at dusk, they are given more food. When it is cold, and throughout the long winters, the animals must stay in the barn. This is difficult for a species used to spending the entire year moving about in a warm climate and dining on fresh leaves every day. Although these giraffes have much more room to roam outside than giraffes in zoos, they have much less room in the barn.

The barn itself is constructed with a high ceiling and eight separate pens where young Safari and the others can be kept separately or in small groups. Some of them are related, so they are used to each other. Their heads stick up above the walls of all the pens and, because they are curious, they always want to know what is going on. All are Rothschild's giraffes, named for Lionel Walter, 2nd Baron Rothschild, who was the famous **zoologist** to first officially describe the giraffe with the distinctive white knee-high socks. While conditions are not ideal in captivity, this subspecies is endangered in the wild, so scientific work with this race is particularly important.

The pens are arranged so that each leads to a passageway that connects the barn with the outside area. As each animal walks along this passage, it comes to the research area where a metal gate prevents it from walking farther. A second gate is closed behind the giraffe so that it must stand still. Then a squeeze bar moves toward the side of the animal's body so that it cannot lunge sideways and get hurt.

Newborn giraffes are able to walk when they are just one hour old and can run shortly after that!

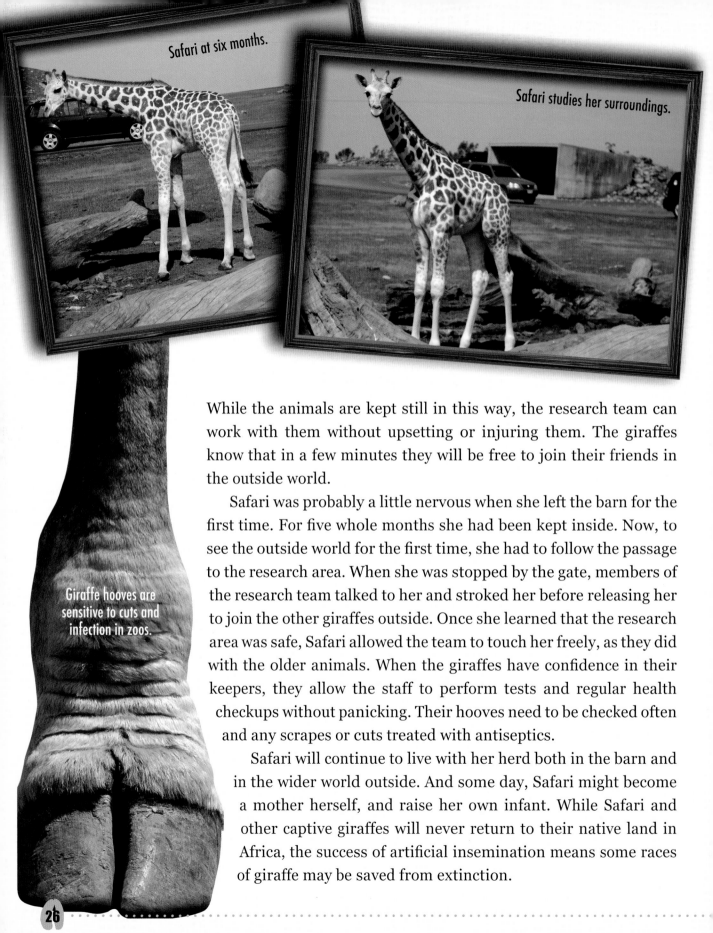

Safari at six months.

Safari studies her surroundings.

Giraffe hooves are sensitive to cuts and infection in zoos.

While the animals are kept still in this way, the research team can work with them without upsetting or injuring them. The giraffes know that in a few minutes they will be free to join their friends in the outside world.

Safari was probably a little nervous when she left the barn for the first time. For five whole months she had been kept inside. Now, to see the outside world for the first time, she had to follow the passage to the research area. When she was stopped by the gate, members of the research team talked to her and stroked her before releasing her to join the other giraffes outside. Once she learned that the research area was safe, Safari allowed the team to touch her freely, as they did with the older animals. When the giraffes have confidence in their keepers, they allow the staff to perform tests and regular health checkups without panicking. Their hooves need to be checked often and any scrapes or cuts treated with antiseptics.

Safari will continue to live with her herd both in the barn and in the wider world outside. And some day, Safari might become a mother herself, and raise her own infant. While Safari and other captive giraffes will never return to their native land in Africa, the success of artificial insemination means some races of giraffe may be saved from extinction.

A giraffe resting in the shade.

HOT AND COLD

HOT WEATHER—WHEW!

Like Safari, giraffes in Canadian zoos and reserves must live inside in winter because they cannot survive in cold weather. In their native Africa, giraffes must be able to survive in both very hot and relatively cold climates. For most animals that live in hot places, the larger they are, the harder it is for them to keep cool. The larger an animal, the more body mass it has where heat is produced, and the relatively smaller body surface it has where this body heat can be released into the environment. Small animals, such as snakes and mice, have a relatively larger body surface from which heat can escape, but even they must stay out of the hot sun, beneath rocks or in burrows, or they would be unable to survive. Giraffes, which are both heavy and live in hot African climates, have evolved a number of ways to deal with the heat.

Most obvious is their shape. When it comes to hot weather, big mammals, such as elephants and hippos, whose bodies are basically barrel-shaped, are even worse off than giraffes, as they have a relatively smaller skin area where cooling can take place. On the hottest days, they

Humans sweat to regulate our temperature. When sweat evaporates from our skin, we cool down.

lounge about in water to beat the heat. A long-legged, lanky giraffe would find it physically difficult to do this. While a tubby hippo might be completely submerged in a cooling water hole, the giraffe might not even get its knees wet! Luckily, it does not need to. The giraffe's elongated shape gives it relatively more skin area where heat can be removed from its body.

Giraffes can keep cool by seeking shade under trees in the wild or inside a building, but they only do this when it is very hot. Even at 37°C (99°F) a giraffe may be content to stand or lie down in full sunlight. In some hot desert areas, giraffes, like camels, will either stand facing toward or away from the sun so that as few of its hot rays as possible fall onto their bodies.

Baby giraffes in the wild are much less able to deal with the heat than adults, which is why their mothers leave them in shady areas in the daytime while they go off in search of food. Small calves do not drink water, perhaps because their legs are too long, or their necks too short, for them to reach down to a pool or river. In any case, if a baby followed its mother into hot open areas, it would be in danger of becoming overheated and dehydrated.

The giraffes' diet helps keep them fit for the weather, too. Because of the hot, dry climate in much of Africa, giraffes eat leaves, which can be as much as sixty percent water. That means that a large male who fills his stomach completely with 34 kilograms (75 pounds) of leaves each day is also taking in 21 litres (44 pints) of water. No wonder he may not need to drink extra water at all!

Some researchers believe that their skin-covered horns may help giraffes cope with hot weather. Blood travels to this skin, where the air cools it. This cooler blood then flows around the brain and back into the giraffe's neck and body. However, if the air temperature is very high, the transfer of heat could go the wrong way and actually make the animal hotter!

Giraffes, unlike people, are able to raise their body temperature as the outside air temperature increases during hot days. Therefore, on hot days when we are sweating to keep cool, giraffes do not need to

The giraffe's long shape allows for heat to escape.

do this. This way they conserve water in their bodies and do not need to drink as much. This is vital in parts of Africa where there are few lakes or rivers. As the day cools in the late afternoon, their body temperature slowly falls again. Although giraffes are physically unable either to pant or sweat, they do have sweat glands in their skin. This tells scientists that their ancestors did sweat when it was hot, but that over time, these glands have become useless because sweating releases a great deal of water from the body, and water itself is limited in the savannah areas that giraffes favour.

Giraffes are not adapted to live in cold climates.

COLD WEATHER—BRRR!

Obviously giraffes are superbly adapted to thrive in hot weather, but what about cold weather? In most places where giraffes live in Africa, it never gets cold. However, giraffes are now being kept captive in cold climates, and their bodies can't adapt to the new weather conditions.

In 1957, for example, many giraffes lived among cattle on a huge ranch in the province of Mpumalanga, in South Africa. The dry season had been long, with little rain, so all the wild animals were in poor condition. One winter weekend the temperature dropped from 30°C (86°F) to 7°C (45°F). Along with this drop came a strong south wind and cold rain. On Monday, twenty-one giraffes lay dead.

Needless to say, giraffes living in zoos in northern climates must be protected in winter. With the stress of cold weather, many captive giraffes have died suddenly, apparently without having been sick. They had been affected by an ailment called **serous fat atrophy**, where deposits of fat in the body are limited and less firm than normal. This had been brought on in part by cold weather and in part by a diet unlike what they would eat in the wild. In Vancouver, Canada, some giraffes have died within the past five years, in part because of the climate there. Despite the stress giraffes undergo during transportation, these giraffes should ideally be shipped south where the climate is much more suitable for them.

Gemina's unusual neck.

CHAPTER 7

BRAVE GEMINA

Excitement was in the air at the spacious San Diego Wild Animal Park in California in 1986 as everyone awaited the birth of a baby Rothschild's giraffe. Since its first discovery more than a century ago, this giraffe subspecies had become endangered in the wild, so the birth of this healthy female, named Gemina, was an especially welcome event.

Gemina spent her early days near her mother, who provided her with milk and motherly attention. She also liked to be with the other young giraffes in the large park. But the city of Santa Barbara wanted Gemina for its zoo, so when she was just eighteen months old, she was forced to leave her mother and friends to move from a large park to a zoo with much smaller quarters. Gemina was loaded into a truck for the 300-kilometre (186-mile) trip. It must have been so confusing and frightening for her. Although she wouldn't have known this, it is also dangerous to move giraffes—sometimes they die of a heart attack during transportation, or from falling down, or from being hurt by an overhead structure. Fortunately, brave Gemina survived the trip.

She soon made friends with the other giraffes in her new home,

A giraffe giving Gemina a kiss.

growing up and up as the months passed until she was more than 4 metres (13.5 feet) tall. But when she was three years old, Gemina developed a bump on the side of her neck. No one knew why, although she had had a fall shortly before the bump was noticed. Or, maybe her bump had somehow been **inherited** from one of her parents. As the years passed, the bump grew larger and larger, until her neck had a bend of almost ninety degrees. No one at the zoo had ever heard of anything like this. Veterinarians who X-rayed her found that several neck bones were misshapen, but they did not know why.

At first, everyone was worried about Gemina. She looked so strange, but she did not seem to be in pain. Each day she joined her friends in eating leaves, fruits, and grains from high baskets set out for them. Because the bend in her neck made her shorter than the other giraffes, her friends sometimes dropped hay on her head as they ate, which made the keepers laugh.

Eventually, Gemina became pregnant. The keepers at the zoo wondered if she would be able to raise a calf like the other female

No one knew why Gemina's neck was crooked.

giraffes did. Her calf was born normally, but died when it was a few months old. Later on, she became pregnant once more, but again the youngster did not live to grow up. No one knew if the problem with her neck had anything to do with her being unable to raise her calves to adulthood.

Visitors loved to come and see Gemina because she was different from the other giraffes. Many people thought she must be the most famous giraffe in the world because they had heard so much about her and her crooked neck in newspapers, or on the radio or television. Once, a young boy who had a bump on his shoulder visited. When he saw Gemina he shouted, "That giraffe has a bump like me!" The boy was happy knowing that Gemina was popular, even though she had a disability. In fact, Gemina made many people with disabilities feel better because, though different, she was so appreciated and accepted.

Gemina lived for a long time at the Santa Barbara Zoo, loved by the many thousands of people who came to see her. When she was twenty-one years old, the zoo held a party in her honour. She was given a huge card decorated with her favourite food and covered with the names of boys and girls who had signed it for her. They all wished her an even longer life. She couldn't read the names, but she could eat the leaves, which she did with great relish. At twenty-one, she was older than most giraffes that live in the wild or in captivity. Her crooked neck had not affected her life span.

But Gemina was growing old. Sometimes when she was tired, she would rest her weary head on a rock wall, which was just the right height. About a year later, after a long and healthy life, brave Gemina died at the zoo.

In her memory, a stone was placed in front of the yard where Gemina lived with her friends for so long. It was dedicated to her, with the inscription: "She showed us differences can be accepted and celebrated." She left a wonderful legacy for all the people who read these words.

Would Gemina have lived a happier life had she been born in the wild or on a reserve? As a young giraffe, she would have travelled with her mother to find leaves to eat and had the freedom to make friends of her own. She would have enjoyed exploring the wonderful savannah areas of Africa where she lived. But if the neck abnormality was genetic, as she grew older and her neck became more crooked, she would have been a target for lions. Predators often attack individuals that are different. Gemina is one of few giraffes lucky enough to have a good life at the zoo among her many friends.

In fact, Gemina made many people with disabilities feel better because, though different, she was so appreciated and accepted.

A giraffe's neck can also extend to reach low bushes.

THE GIRAFFE'S UNUSUAL BODY

Take a good look at that long giraffe neck. How many bones do you think support it? Surprisingly, despite its length, a giraffe neck has only seven bones—the same as a human one. By contrast, long-necked birds, such as swans, have as many as twenty-five neck bones.

The skulls of adult males, which weigh about 10 kilograms (22 pounds), are almost three times as heavy as those of females. This is because only males use their heads in fights, battering an opponent's body with their horns. Because of these battles, males develop bony structures at the back of their skulls, sometimes called mizzen horns, where neck muscles and a strong ligament are attached. Generally, giraffe bones resemble those of other large mammals. Muscles are attached to these bones, which helps keep the neck erect.

Giraffes have thirty-two teeth in all, again like people, but have no upper front teeth or upper **canines**. Instead, the roof of the mouth is a hard **palate**. They press their lower front teeth against the palate to pull leaves into their mouths—with the help of their long tongues. Rather than being sharp, the two lower canines are

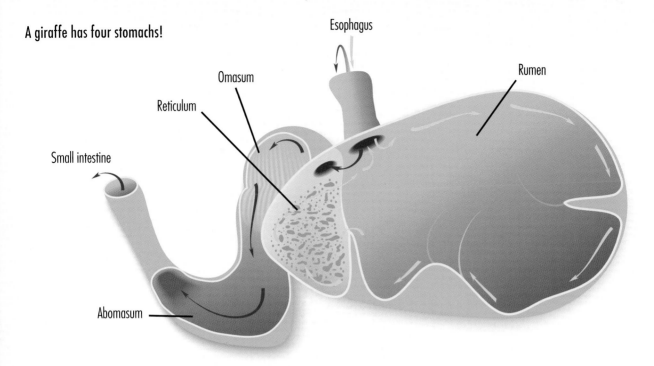

A giraffe has four stomachs!

Esophagus

Omasum

Reticulum

Rumen

Small intestine

Abomasum

flattened out to make the front row of lower teeth wider.

Researchers have found that many giraffes in zoos—but few in the wild—have teeth with a visible flaw in the outer enamel. This defect is caused by stress in the life of a young giraffe, perhaps an early pregnancy in a female, or being bullied for a young male. Because the teeth grow in at different times, researchers can tell from a tooth when a negative event happened. This information will be useful in determining, for example, if a certain diet in a zoo or the transportation of a giraffe from one place to another was stressful to an animal.

While humans have only one stomach, giraffes have four! The first stomach, the large rumen, is where leaves accumulate as a giraffe eats. There, they are mixed with stomach juices and made into boluses, small packets of leaves, which the giraffe **regurgitates** and chews thoroughly when it is at rest. Only water goes into the small second stomach, the reticulum. Once chewed, the bolus then goes down into the third stomach, the omasum or psalterium. In the omasum, the food is manipulated by muscles in the stomach walls and passed to the fourth stomach, the abomasum, where digestive juices mix with the food, which is now liquid (see figure above). In the small intestine, the digested food is passed into the blood stream to be carried to all parts of the body.

A giraffe skeleton.

A giraffe's hooves are extremely hard and flat, with large foot pads to support its huge weight. The front hooves are slightly wider than the back because they have to support more weight, given the giraffe's heavy neck and chest. These well-designed feet serve the animals well in the wild where they may walk for long distances, but are very often a problem in zoos. The hooves tend to become overgrown, so zoo workers have to trim them. This is a challenging operation— if the hooves are cut back incorrectly, it will affect the legs and movement and make it difficult for the giraffe to walk. The trimming process is also traumatic for some individuals, who could die from the stress. This problem is specific to giraffes in captivity because giraffes in the wild and on reserves have much more room to walk about and their hooves are worn down naturally.

A giraffe's heart is huge, weighing as much as 7.8 kilograms (17 pounds). Its very thick, muscular walls make it a highly effective and efficient organ. Efficiency is necessary because some of the blood leaving the heart must be pushed up through arteries to the brain high above it. The blood carries with it oxygen and particles broken down from food. The blood pressure at a giraffe's heart is about twice as great as that of humans because the blood has to be forced high enough to travel up the giraffe's long neck to reach the brain.

The respiratory system is also unique, because air taken into the body must pass through the **trachea**, the long tube in the giraffe's neck, to reach the lungs. Early on, it was thought that because the trachea was so long, it might affect the functioning of the lungs. However, the length does not appear to be a factor, as the respiration of giraffes is similar to that of other large mammals. They breathe in and out about nine times a minute, on average. When the air is warm and when the giraffe is running, it breathes more often.

An adult human breathes about twelve to sixteen times a minute.

A giraffe galloping.

WALK THIS WAY

Giraffes walk differently. It may be weird, but it works for them. Because of their unusual bodies and long legs, they have developed their own method. Shorter hoofed mammals have a general walking pattern that involves keeping only two diagonal legs on the ground below their bodies during part of each stride. This means their bodies are supported at times only by the right front leg and the left back leg, or the left front leg and the right back leg. But shortly after a giraffe's left back leg begins to swing forward, its left front leg does too. If this front leg had not moved, it would have been hit by the one behind. For a short period, the giraffe is supported by its two right legs, and then by its two left legs. This **lateral stance**—two legs on one side of the body—is a less stable position than the diagonal one of most other animals.

If you were to take a movie of a giraffe walking along, and examine the recording frame by frame in sequence, you would see that its neck moves forward and backward in time with the movement of its legs. Its neck swings forward at the same time as its left legs or right

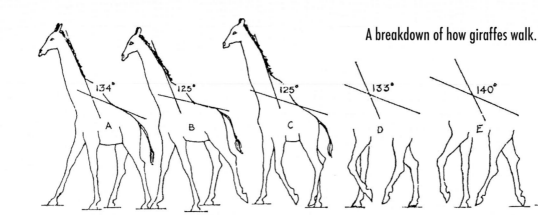

A breakdown of how giraffes walk.

© Anne Innis Dagg

legs. Then the neck pulls back a bit, as if breaking its forward motion, just as these hooves touch the ground again. Giraffes can walk for many kilometres without tiring, sampling the leaves of trees and bushes as they stroll along.

Because of their long legs, giraffes can't **trot**. If they tried to, their back legs would hit their front legs during each stride. Instead, when they want to move quickly, giraffes gallop more or less the way horses do, at speeds of up to 56 kilometres per hour (35 miles per hour). This is fast, but smaller cheetahs and antelopes can run much faster—up to 160 kilometres per hour (100 miles per hour). At a fast gallop, giraffes have all their legs bunched under them in the air once during each stride. But at a slower speed, and for older animals, giraffes may always have at least one hoof on the ground to act as a support and to help keep their balance. Human adults run faster than their children, but with giraffes, it is the youngsters who are the fastest runners. They weigh much less than their parents and have shorter necks, allowing them to gain greater speed.

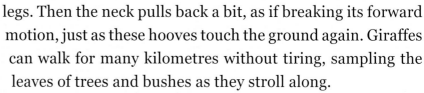

Young giraffes sometimes jump about in play.

Giraffes can keep up a steady gallop for a long time. That's how Lmara and his two pals escaped the lion attack. As long as a giraffe can gallop away before a lion leaps onto its back, it will likely be able to outrun the lion.

Galloping is tiring, though, and makes a giraffe thirsty. In the wet season, giraffes obtain most of the water they need from moisture in the leaves they eat. But in the dry season, they may have to drink at a pool or river. This involves standing next to the water, then leaning

Giraffes must either bend their front legs or spread them far apart to drink from a pond.

down with their front legs either bent or spread far apart, as if they are trying to do the splits. Otherwise, because their legs are so long, their mouths wouldn't be able to reach the water.

Young giraffes can lie down and get up again easily, but as they grow taller, these movements become more difficult. Very old giraffes may never lie down at all. To lie down, a giraffe first folds up its front legs so they are bent under its body, then folds its back legs so it is finally on the ground. It rests on its chest, with its legs sticking out to the right or left of its body. That's relatively easy. Getting up again is harder. The animal throws its neck back so it is able to rest on its **foreknees**. Then it pauses for an instant before swinging its neck forward, this time so its back hooves can be set on the ground. After another pause, the giraffe gives its neck a final lurch back so that the animal can stand on its front feet. Large giraffes may lie down in open areas to rest in the daytime, but they have to be cautious. It takes even a quick giraffe at least four seconds to get up from a resting position and be ready to flee. And if there are lions around, that may just be four seconds too long.

Young giraffes can easily get up from this position, while older giraffes find it harder.

The sequence of how a giraffe gets up from a resting position.

F008 at Soysambu Conservancy.

CHAPTER 10

F008: A MOTHER'S LOVE

Zoe Muller, head of the Rothschild's Giraffe Project in Kenya, was making her regular morning drive around the 60,000-acre Soysambu Conservancy, looking to see what the giraffes were up to. Usually she would see in the distance perhaps eleven individuals at one time—maybe several males involved in a battle or other animals lying down and chewing their food. Today, she saw an infant bouncing from one female to another, each bending down to touch the youngster on the head. This young giraffe was obviously enjoyed by all of the females, even though only one of them was its mother. By touching the baby, they seemed to be welcoming it into their group.

Scores of wild animals—herds of buffaloes, zebras, gazelles, and baboons—roam in this sanctuary, where they can live out their lives as nature intended. Giraffes are constantly on the move, choosing to browse from one type of tree and then another much farther away. Sometimes they hang out with relatives, and sometimes with individuals they have seldom met. There's no stress brought on by freezing temperatures or lack of stimulation. Zoe watched a group

Female giraffes, like F008 pictured here, usually stay together in groups.

of Rothschild's giraffes wander over to drink from a small lake. Because this race of giraffe is facing extinction in other countries from hunters, many individual giraffes were transported to this sanctuary for protection.

Wanting to learn everything she could about them, Zoe kept a file on each individual. Naming individual giraffes was an important part of her early research on their behaviours. All giraffes have a one-of-a-kind spotting pattern on their coats, as unique to them as a human fingerprint is to us. While working with photographs, Zoe would soon learn to recognize and name every giraffe she encountered in the conservancy. That made it easier for her to follow the adventures of the individuals from day to day, and year to year.

One of these giraffes was named F008, the eighth giraffe officially recognized by Zoe. Through her binoculars, Zoe spotted her, standing in a cluster with sixteen other females. What was going on? Soon, Zoe realized that F008 and the others were focusing their attention on F008's dead baby. Not wanting to disturb them, Zoe backed up her vehicle and settled down to watch what was happening from a distance.

Two weeks earlier, F008 had given birth to her first calf. She had nursed and looked after her infant as well as she could, but it had

> **Elephants mourn their dead in different ways. Some do so by touching or even burying the bones of the deceased elephant.**

Infrasound
(below 16 Hz)

Audible frequencies
(16 Hz – 20kHz)

Ultrasound
(over 20kHz)

Infrasound is a method of communication carried through the ground.

died of natural causes. Now it seemed that F008 did not want to leave her offspring as it lay still on the ground, no longer responsive to her care. We have known for years that elephants, gorillas, and chimpanzees **mourn** their dead, but it was assumed that giraffes and other hoofed animals were not intelligent or sensitive enough to grieve.

In fact, in the 1960s, biologists didn't think giraffes were social animals. From one week to the next, females were seen with new acquaintances rather than with their pals from the week before. If a group of females was seen feeding together on the leaves of some acacia trees, it was assumed they were only together because there were plenty of leaves there to eat. Longer-term studies have shown that females do stay together much more often than previously thought. Scientists think that they may communicate with each other by infrasound, vocal noises that can travel long distances but are so low that they cannot be heard by human ears. If so, giraffes that are far apart may still be in communication with each other.

Usually, when a young giraffe dies, its mother stays nearby for a few hours, and then moves on with her life, leaving her baby's body behind. What else could she do? But this was different.

For the next three hours, Zoe watched as F008 and her distressed friends moved back and forth and in circles, often approaching the dead baby to reach down and nudge it with their muzzles. Zoe was so amazed at their unusual behaviour that she returned several times later during the day. By late afternoon, there were even more giraffes in that spot, all still surrounding the dead calf. No giraffe was feeding, which would have been their usual activity at that time of day. What better evidence that these females really were friends that supported each other!

Zoe drove to the same area each morning for the next few days to record the giraffes' behaviours. There were fewer giraffes on the second day, and by the third day, only F008 was left. The next day the body of the baby was gone, but F008 still stayed. All alone, she remained in the area for several more days, rare for females, who prefer to stay in groups. F008 was grieving the death of the youngster she had nursed for such a short time. She became famous when her devotion was reported in newspapers around the world and on the Internet. Because of Zoe's careful work, F008 would become the first famous wild giraffe.

Soon, because of Zoe's description of F008's unusual behaviour, other giraffe researchers in Africa began reporting similar events with giraffes that they had observed. In 2013, Zoe and Megan Strauss, who for years researched Maasai giraffes in Tanzania, wrote a scientific paper about the devotion female giraffes had for their dead infants. The paper observed behaviours of five different races. Strangely, the behaviour had not been reported before in the 200 years that explorers and settlers had lived near giraffes in Africa. Obviously, to learn everything about the behaviours of a wild animal, researchers have to spend years carefully observing and documenting all its activities. It is only in the wild that such behavioural characteristics can be seen and documented.

Zoe is excited to report that F008, who is now six or seven years old, gave birth to a baby girl in April 2014. We hope that this youngster will live to grow to adulthood, to enjoy the spacious land where she lives, and to help keep the Rothschild's race from becoming extinct in the wild.

F008 with her second calf.

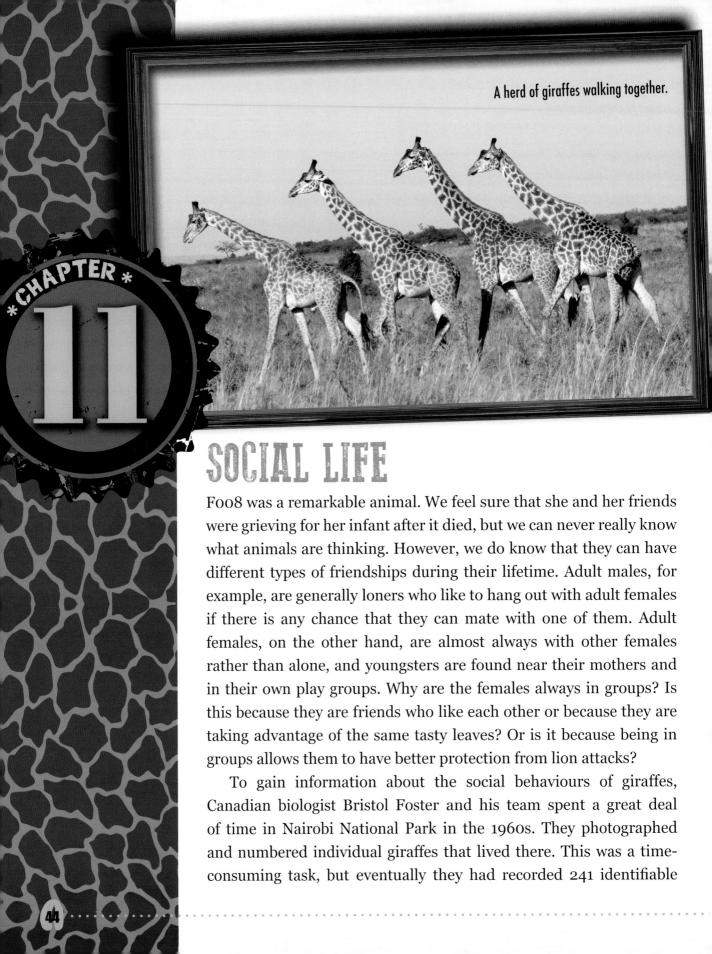

A herd of giraffes walking together.

SOCIAL LIFE

F008 was a remarkable animal. We feel sure that she and her friends were grieving for her infant after it died, but we can never really know what animals are thinking. However, we do know that they can have different types of friendships during their lifetime. Adult males, for example, are generally loners who like to hang out with adult females if there is any chance that they can mate with one of them. Adult females, on the other hand, are almost always with other females rather than alone, and youngsters are found near their mothers and in their own play groups. Why are the females always in groups? Is this because they are friends who like each other or because they are taking advantage of the same tasty leaves? Or is it because being in groups allows them to have better protection from lion attacks?

To gain information about the social behaviours of giraffes, Canadian biologist Bristol Foster and his team spent a great deal of time in Nairobi National Park in the 1960s. They photographed and numbered individual giraffes that lived there. This was a time-consuming task, but eventually they had recorded 241 identifiable giraffes. During a twenty-month period, Bristol and his crew drove around the large park once a week, recording the identities of all the giraffes they encountered, who they were with, and what they were doing.

A group of giraffes sticking together.

What they found at the end of their study was interesting. Although the females had seemed to be friendly, individuals, seen one week with some giraffes, were almost always with different giraffes the following week and the week after that. During the long-term study, one female was seen with another specific female only 3.4 times. Bristol concluded that giraffes were not really social animals. Over the next forty years, other studies in the wild produced similar results.

Everyone believed this for almost fifty years. Then, American Meredith Bashaw decided to study possible friendships among female giraffes living in the large San Diego Wild Animal Park. She carried out research that was similar to Bristol's, but found that some females were especially friendly with other females. Some twosomes liked to spend time together at a feeding station or when they were resting. Even so, this result for giraffes in captivity might differ from that in the wild. Maybe such friendships occurred because there was not much room for giraffes to be far apart from each other. Or could it be that captivity itself changed giraffe behaviour? Further research was needed.

Now, extensive studies, such as that of Australian Kerryn Carter who identified 535 individual giraffes in Namibia, indicate that these Namibian giraffes clearly are more social than Bristol Foster had found in Nairobi National Park. Over a six-year period, Kerryn and her team drove the roads where the giraffes wandered. By analyzing her data, Kerryn found that some of these females did hang out with special friends over the course of at least six years. Sometimes this was true of a mother and her daughter.

We now think that giraffes may communicate through infrasound. Individuals may have a number of close friendships that we know nothing about because they are based on activities we cannot hear or see. A female could be telling her oldest daughter that she is feeding on an acacia tree over the next hill. Her daughter could be answering that she and her infant will join her in a short while, after she visits a pool for a drink of water. But a person might assume that, because they were apart, these two giraffes were not friends at all.

Giraffes are now known to have a social lifestyle in the wild that is entirely different to what they must endure in zoos. In their native areas in Africa, females like to be together at times, but often go from one group to another in the course of a few days. This is called a fission/fusion mode of living. But wherever they are, unknown to us, they may be in contact through infrasound communication. Humans have the same sort of friendships. We spend time with those we know through school or sports, but we also like to be alone sometimes. We can keep in touch with others not by infrasound, but with cell phones.

Giraffes aren't as social as other animals, such as elephants, though. No group stays together all the time. Giraffes like to wander off wherever they can find tasty food, and then later reunite with others. Aimee Nelson of Indiana's Fort Wayne Children's Zoo carried out research on infrasound behaviour on the giraffes in her care. Her early observations indicate that an animal sending an infrasound message points his or her head straight up into the air. Or a male may bend his neck far back, as the large one does in her zoo. This seems to happen if a female is ready to mate. We do not know exactly what communication passes between two animals. This is a fascinating area that needs much more research.

A family of giraffes at the Cheyenne Mountain Zoo.

CLEVER MSITU

Five-year-old Msitu loves to have visitors at the Cheyenne Mountain Zoo in Colorado where she lives, but she isn't always just hanging around to watch the passing parade of people who come to see her. Twice a week she goes to "school" where zoo staff members work with her to keep her life interesting.

There are two kinds of zoos for giraffes and other wild animals. In one type, the zookeepers believe that their animals must be allowed, as much as possible, to live as they would in nature, even though they are in captivity. They believe that the animals should not interact with human beings because they do not do so in the wild. Unfortunately, captive giraffes live in small enclosures and can easily become bored. The variety of food is limited and their fellow giraffes are always the same. So, in the second type of zoo, the staff members feel that wild animals deserve to have a life that is as stimulating as possible.

In the past, when all zoos seemed like prisons, a giraffe would have been bored stiff with its life. There would have been little for

Msitu and friends.

her to do but stand around and wait for food to arrive. Many bored giraffes resort to weird behaviours, such as licking fences, waving their tongues around, or pacing endlessly back and forth. These strange acts are called **stereotypies**, and they only occur in zoo animals. Many zoo animals lack mental stimulation in captivity. In the wild or on reserves, a female giraffe can roam for long distances, forage for tasty leaves, hang out with other females or young giraffes, and have the freedom to enjoy whatever nature has to offer.

Msitu's keepers work with her and the other giraffes, using food rewards to teach them new things to brighten their days and keep their minds and senses active. Giraffes are sensitive and nervous by nature. At another zoo, giraffes were traumatized once when a zebra accidentally kicked a blue ball into their paddock. They rushed into the giraffe house and refused to come out again for the rest of the week. By learning new activities with a staff member, a giraffe becomes confident instead of nervous. Staff members from zoos all over North America come to this facility to learn more about making life more interesting for captive giraffes. However, many zoos try but fail to provide all the activities for their giraffes to thrive.

Some learning is easy because it is straightforward. By watching other giraffes, Msitu quickly discovered how to pull food from baskets with her tongue—baskets with sweet potatoes, carrots, green beans, and often a few bananas. When she was thirsty, she learned to drink from water containers and an outside pond.

Msitu began learning about life in a zoo when she was very young. She picked up new ideas quickly, even though she was cautious at first of new people and anything that she had not seen before. When she correctly performed a specific activity, she was rewarded with a cracker, romaine lettuce, or a tree branch. And, of course, she was never punished for any reason.

Now, twice a week, Msitu continues to work on a variety of behaviours with her primary staff member. She willingly stands on a scale so she can be weighed, and she is so clever that she has learned to respond to requests such as "move up" and "back up" so the staff members can monitor her health more easily.

Because she learned these behaviours, keepers know how to help her when she needs it. One day, on a "move in" command, she lined up to a barrier where the veterinary crew, using a "touch" cue, were able to do an **ultrasound** on her body. This test showed that Msitu was pregnant. The staff was then able to take extra care of her, adding supplements to her daily food and placing her in a sand stall when she was about to give birth. The sand on the floor acted as a cushion when her infant daughter, Emy, fell to the ground at birth.

When Msitu is not feeling well, her past learning comes into play. It helps her to stand still rather than panic when she is given an injection or when blood is drawn. Without preparation, she would be too scared to be examined. She would have to be given an **anaesthetic** so veterinarians could find out what was wrong with her. This procedure can be both stressful and dangerous for giraffes and sometimes can cause life-threatening complications.

Her learned confidence is also useful when it comes to foot and leg care. Like our fingernails, a giraffe's hooves keep growing throughout its life, so they have to be trimmed regularly. If a vet wants Msitu to put her right front hoof onto a block, he or she says the word "right." Then Msitu plants her right hoof there so it can be carefully cut back. If there are any small stones stuck in her hoof, they

Some zoos in England used the bloodsucking kissing bug to withdraw blood from zoo animals, such as giraffes. The kissing bugs release a pain-reducing enzyme and can get a blood sample from the giraffe in a stress-free way.

A female giraffe has her hoof cared for at the Cheyenne Mountain Zoo.

can be removed before they cause pain and limping. Msitu is also comfortable standing still for an X-ray if there are other possible hoof problems. Because giraffes do much less walking in captivity than they do in the wild, and often step on cement or other hard surfaces, many of them suffer from problems such as **laminitis**.

Many giraffes in zoos also suffer from various other medical problems that are rare or unknown in the wild. Some—like indigestion or unnatural wearing of the teeth—may be because of the food they eat, which is not their natural diet. Captive giraffes often suffer from arthritis, **rickets**, bone fractures, heart attacks, **tuberculosis, pneumonia**, and **listeriosis**.

Luckily, giraffes seem to enjoy the mental stimulation of learning with a human. During her sessions, Msitu sometimes works with different staff members. This exposes her to new people, using new methods. Being familiar with a variety of people and possibilities makes her more relaxed and better able to enjoy her captive life at the zoo.

Giraffes like Msitu are willing to interact with the public to some extent. Visitors can purchase healthy giraffe food to feed them, and they can watch most of the learning sessions to see how the staff members go about their work and how the giraffes respond. The managers of the Cheyenne Mountain Zoo hope that zoos everywhere will begin learning programs with their giraffes because it gives their lives more meaning in captivity. The least humans can do is create activities to keep captive animals as mentally and physically stimulated as possible. You only have to watch happy Msitu to agree.

A giraffe and a visitor connect.

Buddy and his twin sister, Wasswa.

SEEING DOUBLE

The owners of the Natural Bridge Wildlife Ranch near San Antonio, Texas, had a surprise in store for them when eight-year-old reticulated giraffe, Carol, was ready to give birth on May 10, 2013. They were delighted with the arrival of Wasswa, a lovely baby female. But they were amazed when her brother appeared, feet first, some minutes later! A few twin giraffes have been born in the wild and in captivity over many years, but almost never have both survived. Luckily, because twenty giraffes had been born at this ranch over many years, the staff knew how best to provide care for the infant twins.

Although the staff members were excited about the rare births, they were also worried about the twins' health. They held a hurried conference about what to do: Would Carol have enough milk to raise two babies successfully? Would Wasswa, who was smaller than her brother, be able to compete with him for their mother's milk? At their time of birth, Wasswa was 1.4 metres (4.5 feet) tall, weighing 43 kilograms (95 pounds), while her brother, Buddy, was 1.7 metres (5.6 feet) tall and weighed 57 kilograms (125 pounds). The staff knew

A giraffe grows a metre taller in its first year.

that it's always best for a baby giraffe to be raised by its mother, but if Carol didn't have enough milk for both her calves, neither would thrive, and both might die.

They finally decided that it would be safest to have little Wasswa raised by her mother, while stronger Buddy would be bottle-fed by the staff. Wasswa stayed close to her mother, sucking milk whenever she felt like it, just as all giraffe young do in the wild. By contrast, Buddy's caregivers had to quickly give him colostrum, the fluid produced at birth by new mothers, which is rich in antibodies and minerals, to keep him healthy. Then they set up a system that involved constantly preparing bottles of warmed cow's milk to hold above Buddy so that he could suckle. At first he was fed every few hours, night and day, just like human newborns, which kept the staff busy.

As he grew older, Buddy was cut down to three drinking sessions a day; by that time he was old enough to munch on some of the food prepared for the older giraffes, such as grain, leaves, and hay. The staff was on constant alert to make sure Buddy remained healthy, given his unnatural diet. In the wild, of course, he would have been nibbling at leaves when he was several months old. Gradually, he would have added more and more types of leaves to his diet to obtain the best possible nourishment.

Despite the unusual arrangements that had been necessary for the twins, they both fared well physically as they grew older. A

Buddy greets Anne, the author.

year later, Wasswa was 2.9 metres (9.5 feet) tall and her brother was 2.8 metres (9.3 feet) tall.

Had they been born and lived in the African wilderness and survived, at the age of two, Wasswa would perhaps still be near her mother, while Buddy would have teamed up with other young males his age. He and the boys probably would have been having sparring matches, hitting each other with their horns, just as Lmara was doing in northern Kenya at the same age.

Because the twins were born in the Natural Bridge Wildlife Ranch and by necessity raised under unnatural conditions, Wasswa behaves quite differently from Buddy. She is not interested in any of the people who visit outside their large enclosure, whereas Buddy, who has had far more contact with people, is much less nervous. He remains fond of the staff members who acted for so long as his substitute mother in providing milk for him. He and Wasswa are the only twin giraffes in the United States.

A new invention allows scientists to recognize every giraffe they encounter because of their unique patterns.

CHAPTER 14

RESEARCHING GIRAFFES TO SAVE THEM

When I sailed to Africa to study giraffes in 1956 and 1957, I was lucky. So little was known about my favourite animal in the wild that everything I would later report about them was new to science. No one had documented their normal activities in their native land. Not that this was unusual at the time, because no scientist had studied the activities of any other African animals, either. Jane Goodall's work observing chimpanzees would not begin for another four years. I had to pay my own way, but today, students can earn fellowships or other awards that enable them to carry out original research, working along with experienced investigators.

What cutting-edge scientific research has been done recently on giraffes? Here are two recent examples.

POPULATION STUDIES

Douglas Bolger, a professor at New Hampshire's Dartmouth College, and his colleagues have developed a computer program that allows them to recognize every giraffe that they encounter. This is possible

It is illegal to kill a giraffe in Niger.

because, as we have seen, each animal has its own unique pattern of spotting. Field scientists no longer have to leaf through hundreds of photographs to determine which individual they are observing.

This new invention allows scientists and students to drive through large regions, take snapshots of all the individual giraffes they encounter, and return to the lab to enter the data into the program. Every few months, they can drive the same network of roads to photograph all the giraffes they see again. From the vast amount of information they have collected, the researchers can document how many giraffes live in each area and to what extent the animals move from one area to another. They can even determine the survival rate of specific groups of giraffes.

These data can then be linked with such things as rainfall, time of year, and human activity. Human activity is of particular interest, because where many people live in poverty, giraffes are likely to be killed for food. If giraffes are to survive, guardians must be sent to such places to protect the animals. This new program allows researchers to know exactly where to send guardians for protection.

● Where *G.c. peralta* are left
◐ Where *G.c. peralta* used to roam

SAVING THE WEST AFRICAN GIRAFFE

Over the last hundred years, the number of giraffes belonging to the *Giraffa camelopardalis peralta* race in Africa has declined drastically. Giraffes of this race used to live in many countries in northwest Africa—in Gambia, Mauritania, Senegal, Mali, Nigeria, and Niger. Now they exist only in Niger. This dry country, one of the poorest in the world, does not have the resources to set up reserves where giraffes can live in safety. Rather, giraffes and people survive in close quarters. A village woman hanging out laundry to dry may turn her head to see a giraffe walking by. Some giraffes even gather in areas that cattle frequent and near where crops are grown.

By 1996, the *G.c. peralta* race of giraffes in Niger was almost extinct. Poaching had become so widespread that only fifty individuals of this race remained. Other countries that had lost their giraffes had made little effort to try to save them. But the people of Niger decided to do things differently. Their government passed laws banning all killing of giraffes and cutting down trees that supply them with food. As well, a local group set up the Association to Safeguard the Giraffes of Niger (ASGN), financed by both local people and those living outside the country and continent. This group carried out various research studies to determine how to save and increase the giraffe population in Niger.

The goals of the ASGN were to educate local people about their long-necked friends, to carry out research on the giraffes, to take a census each year of their numbers, and to provide aid to villagers living in the zone frequented by giraffes. These people soon realized that keeping giraffes safe had beneficial results, because ASGN aid included digging wells to make life easier for the locals and loaning them money. One woman bought sheep and goats with an ASGN loan, which she fattened up and sold for a profit. "Giraffes have brought happiness here," she said. "Their presence brings us lots of things."

From 1996 to 1999, there was a very high birth rate, and since then, there has been a steady increase of giraffes. By 2012, there were estimated to be about 310 giraffes in Niger. This number is well on the way to the target of 400 adult giraffes, which is thought to be enough to ensure the future of the population. Most people in Niger are thrilled with this success story, although the road ahead is still difficult.

Conservations and reserves must be built to protect endangered giraffes.

CHAPTER

HELP WANTED: SAVING GIRAFFES

WILD GIRAFFES

The simple truth is that giraffes in Africa are in danger of having no future. Some races that live in desert areas where there are few people are doing well—in Namibia and other parts of southern Africa, for instance—but most giraffe races in the wild are threatened with extinction.

Many years ago, giraffes died only from natural causes. If lions were prevalent in an area, some giraffes were killed by these predators. Diseases also wiped out many more. Giraffes almost never died during drought because they could walk long distances to other areas to find food and water.

In recent years, though, the human population in Africa has been increasing rapidly, expanding into areas that once belonged to giraffes and other wild animals. Only in Niger do people and wild giraffes live together peacefully. Elsewhere, giraffes are too often hunted and killed for sport and food. When human beings and their cattle take over giraffe terrain, the giraffes may be driven out or exterminated. Agricultural lands tend to be fenced these days, which may trap giraffes either inside, such as on cattle ranches, or outside, away from the trees where they could find food.

A taxonomist determines whether an animal is a full species or a subspecies, now based on DNA samples. One way to tell the difference is that subspecies (of the same species) are able to interbreed while creatures of different species cannot.

HELPING TO CONSERVE GIRAFFES IN THE WILD

Unless measures are put into place to conserve giraffes in the wild, some races will surely become extinct. The International Union for the Conservation of Nature (IUCN) is considering further protection for them beyond the two races already designated endangered: *G.c. peralta* in Niger and *G.c. rothschildi* in Kenya and Uganda. The Union will determine if some or all of the nine recognized subspecies of giraffes are different enough to be considered full species. If so, the need to conserve them would intensify.

Several organizations are already working to prevent the extinction of all the distinct groups of giraffes in Africa, be they subspecies or full species. These include the Giraffe Conservation Alliance and the IUCN's Giraffe and Okapi Specialist Group (GOSG).

CAPTIVE GIRAFFES

In a perfect world, there would be no zoos. Animals would live out their lives in their own habitats, free to roam, eat, and make friends as they wish. But the world is not perfect. Long ago, animals from foreign lands were transported to cities and towns where people paid money to see them. There were no television sets or movies then, so viewing and learning about strange animals was exciting. Zoos became big business.

Of course, learning about wild animals is important. Otherwise, people could be hunting a species to extinction and few people would realize or care about the issue. But with today's technological advances,

Zoo giraffes are confined to small areas with fences.

such as movies, television, and the Internet, there is no need to remove animals from the wild to admire and learn about them.

Wild animals should live in the wild rather than in captivity. Zoos are simply too small for animals to live in naturally, and those up north have much too cold a climate. But we know that if we released zoo animals back into their natural habitat, many would suffer and die. They would not be able to cope with transportation, new diets, predators, and surroundings unfamiliar to them. The best solution for zoo animals, such as giraffes, is to send them to large reserves or conservancies established in their natural climates. There they could roam about and live out their lives as their ancestors did, taking long walks from one cluster of trees to another and hanging out with changing groups of others of their kind, rather than living in a never-changing confined zoo area with one set of individuals for life.

HOW TO BECOME A GIRAFFE GUARDIAN

- Check out zoos before you visit them. Are they large enough to give their animals lots of room to move about? Do they have a good reputation for animal care? Do not support or visit **roadside zoos**.
- Organize festivals to honour World Giraffe Day, which began on June 21, 2014, to celebrate the animal with the longest neck on the longest day of the year! At the festival, advertise information about the need to save giraffes from extinction and captivity.
- Raise money to send to the conservation groups listed earlier or to the Reticulated Giraffe Project. The donations will be used to help prevent poachers from killing giraffes and to react to emergency situations, such as a war.
- Send letters expressing your interest in giraffes to any groups that might be persuaded to help them.
- Raise awareness by letting your friends and family know that the giraffes' future is at risk.
- Create a Facebook page, website, or blog to help spread the word.

GLOSSARY

Anaesthetic: a drug or gas given to an individual to cause loss of sensation

Ancestor: an individual from which other genetically related individuals come

Artificial insemination: a method of introducing sperm into the uterus of the female so she can produce a baby

Biologist: a person trained to study animals and plants

Breed: to mate in order to produce offspring

Browsing: eating the leaves of trees and bushes rather than grass

Bush meat: meat from animals that have been killed illegally

Calf/calves: the young of certain animals, such as giraffes

Canines: enlarged teeth at the outside corners of the front row of teeth; while most mammals' canines are long and sharp, giraffe canines are rounded and wide to make grabbing leaves easier

Climate: the prevailing weather conditions of a place

DNA (deoxyribonucleic acid): the material that carries genetic information that makes individuals distinct

Endangered category: official category of the International Union for the Conservation of Nature, which indicates that special measures must be taken to protect a subspecies or species

Evolve: gradual change in a group that over time leads to new groups

Extinction: the destruction of every member of a species or subspecies so that it no longer exists on Earth

Fly switch: a tail or other utensil used to shoo away flies

Foreknees: joints halfway up the legs of the giraffe

Game hunter: a person who hunts and kills large wild animals

Herbivore: an animal that feeds only on plants

Hoof/hooves: the horny feet of many large mammals

Import: to bring from another place

Inherit: passing genetic material from a parent to its young

Interbreed: breeding between two different classes or groups, such as between subspecies/races

Laminitis: inflammation of the sensitive part of an animal's hoof

Lateral stance: two feet either on the right or on the left side supporting an animal at any one time

Mammal: any warm-blooded animal species with females who give birth to and suckle their young

Massacre: the killing of many individuals

Maternal instincts: a bond that forms between a mother and her baby

Mate: the connecting of a male and female so that young can be produced

Mourn: to grieve

Naturalist: any person who enjoys and studies nature

Okapi: the only living relative of the giraffe

Ossicones: the horns on a giraffe made of bone covered with skin

Palate: roof of the mouth

Pica behaviour: eating substances, such as soil or bones, which are not considered food

Pliocene period: a period in time that took place 5.3 million to 2.6 million years ago

Pneumonia: an infection that causes the lungs to inflame

Poacher: a person who kills animals illegally

Predator: an animal that kills and eats other animals

Primitive: early or original form

Regurgitate: to bring up food from the stomach back into the mouth

Reserve: land set aside for wild animals where they are protected from hunters

Rickets: a bone disease caused by poor diet

Roadside zoos: facilities where animals are exhibited in small inappropriate cages

Serous fat atrophy: a potentially life-threatening disease in giraffes caused by unnatural diet and/or cold weather

Species: a group of animals or plants that usually breed only among themselves

Stereotypies: abnormal behaviours related to boredom in captive animals

Tendons: strong cords that attach muscle to bone

Theory: an explanation of something that has not been proven but that is generally believed to be true

Trachea: a tube filled with air extending from the nose or mouth to the lungs

Trot: a gait that is faster than a walk but slower than a gallop, in which the body is supported on the ground by diagonal hooves

Tuberculosis: an infectious disease that affects the tissues of the body, especially the lungs

Ultrasound: a painless medical procedure that takes pictures of internal organs

War-torn area: a place such as South Sudan or Sudan where armed soldiers are fighting, causing areas to be unsafe for people and animals

Zoologist: a person trained to study animals

INDEX

BIBLIOGRAPHY

Dagg, Anne Innis. 2006. *Pursuing Giraffe: A 1950s Adventure.* Waterloo, ON: Wilfrid Laurier
  University Press.

Dagg, Anne Innis. 2014. *Giraffe: Biology, Behaviour and Conservation.* Cambridge, UK: Cambridge
  University Press.

Dagg, Anne Innis and Foster, J. Bristol. 1976, 1982. *The Giraffe: Its Biology, Behavior, and Ecology.*
  New York: Van Nostrand Reinhold.

Winnick, Karen B. 2013. *Gemina: The Crooked-Neck Giraffe.* Santa Barbara: Santa Barbara
  Zoological Gardens.

IMAGE CREDITS

TITLE PAGE
Giraffe with tongue out—Copyright Matthew Orselli. Used under license from Shutterstock.com

TABLE OF CONTENTS
Acacia tree—Copyright Graeme Shannon. Used under license from Shutterstock.com

FOREWORD
p. 6   Giraffe eating leaf—Copyright Lee Yiu Tung. Used under license from Shutterstock.com
p. 7   Zoocheck logo—Courtesy of Zoocheck

CHAPTER 1
p. 8   Lmara with zebra—Courtesy of John Doherty
p. 9   Giraffe skin—Copyright anekoho. Used under license from Shutterstock.com
p. 9   Lion eating giraffe—Copyright bjogroet. Used under license from Shutterstock.com
p. 9   Zebra—Copyright Paul Dymott. Used under license from Shutterstock.com
p. 10   Giraffe eating leaf—Copyright Lee Yiu Tung. Used under license from Shutterstock.com
p. 10   Lmara with bird—Courtesy of Anne Innis Dagg
p. 10   Lmara's defining mark—Courtesy of John Doherty
p. 11   Ranger Perspectives—Copyright Jeff Smith. Used under license from Shutterstock.com
p. 11   Lmara reaching up—Courtesy of John Doherty

CHAPTER 2
p. 12   Giraffes browsing—Copyright Chantal de Bruijne. Used under license from Shutterstock.com
p. 13   Giraffe under tree—Copyright Eric Eisnaugle. Used under license from Shutterstock.com
p. 13   Giraffe with tongue in nose—Copyright Nagel Photography. Used under license from Shutterstock.com
p. 14   Stinging ants—Copyright Angel DiBilio. Used under license from Shutterstock.com
p. 15   Grazing giraffe—Copyright Johan Swanepoel. Used under license from Shutterstock.com

CHAPTER 3
p. 16   Mother and baby giraffe—Copyright Athol Abrahams. Used under license from Shutterstock.com
p. 17   Giraffe ancestors—Courtesy of Jean Stevenson
p. 18   Okapi—Copyright Eric Isselee. Used under license from Shutterstock.com
p. 18   Map of giraffe species in 1971—Courtesy of Anne Innis Dagg
p. 19   Thornicoft giraffe—Copyright Johan W. Elzenga. Used under license from Shutterstock.com

CHAPTER 4
p. 20   Giraffe on prehistoric rock—Copyright TanArt. Used under license from Shutterstock.com
p. 21   Giraffe print on suitcase—Copyright Micha Klootwijk. Used under license from Shutterstock.com
p. 22   Hunter chasing giraffes—Copyright Marzolino. Used under license from Shutterstock.com

CHAPTER 5
p. 23   Safari drinking milk—Courtesy of Anne Innis Dagg
p. 24   Mother giraffe cuddling baby—Copyright Henk Bentlage. Used under license from Shutterstock.com
p. 25   Giraffe eating in captivity—Copyright Ilona Ignatova. Used under license from Shutterstock.com
p. 26   Giraffe hoof—Copyright PicturesWild. Used under license from Shutterstock.com
p. 26   Safari and her surroundings—Courtesy of Anne Innis Dagg
p. 26   Safari at six months—Courtesy of Anne Innis Dagg